Green Poems
for a Blue Planet

For Serafina, Luka, and Zita

Green Poems
for a Blue Planet

Martin Kiszko

Illustrations by Nick Park

redcliffe

Acknowledgements

On completing *Green Poems for a Blue Planet* I did wonder whether I was now the creator of a strange new school of poetry – 'Bioverse' – and indeed whether such a collection could ever find its natural habitat in the great forest of literature out there. I am indebted, therefore, to the following friends and colleagues who have helped the poems to find their place in the green debate. My agent Lucy Fawcett and her colleague Gaia Banks for their encouragement and help with editing and contractual matters. My sincere thanks to scientist Frances Arnold who, after hearing me read a few of these poems over breakfast in a New York restaurant, set up the first reading of *Green Poems for a Blue Planet* in Los Angeles in 2009. I am also indebted to Nick Park for his wonderful drawings as well as his enthusiasm and encouragement as I mind-boggled my way in interpreting green issues through the medium of poetry.

Finally, I wish to express my thanks to my publisher John Sansom for his support, guidance and vision to publish the poems. Oh... and then there are all the adults, teenagers and children who listened to me trying out the test-reading of the poems. Thanks for asking the right questions, laughing in the right places and especially for saying '...you know you should really put all those into a book.'   *Martin Kiszko*

First published in 2010 by Redcliffe Press Ltd, 81g Pembroke Road, Bristol, BS8 3EA, UK

www.redcliffepress.co.uk
email: info@redcliffepress.co.uk

ISBN 978-1-906593-55-1

British Library Cataloguing-in-Publication Data:
A catalogue record for this book is available from
The British Library

Cover illustration by Nick Park; cover and book design by Simon Bishop.
Typesetting by Harpertype. Printed in the Czech Republic via Akcent Media.

FSC
Mixed Sources
Product group from well-managed
forests and other controlled sources

Cert no. SW-COC-003532
www.fsc.org
©1996 Forest Stewardship Council

Contents

Takeaway Carbon

Take a step, take a stride,
Take a unicycle ride,
Take a horse that likes the turf,
Take a board to ride the surf.
Take a pogo, take a hop,
Take a long jump, take a bop,
Take a rowboat, walk a lane,
Take the tube, take the train.
Take an elephant, take a mule,
Take a camel to your school,
Take a buggy, take a pram,
Take a donkey, take a tram.
Take a troika, take a sled,
Take a trolley, roll a bed,
Take a team of husky dogs,
Take a set of rolling logs.
Take a jog, take an amble,
Take a jaunt, take a ramble,
Take a skateboard, take a bike,
Take a saunter, take a hike.
Take a ghost ship, trike, or scooter,
Take a go-cart and a hooter,
Take a wagon, take a tandem,
Take a route you wend at random.
Take a kayak or canoe,
Take a ski or take snowshoes,
Take a punt, take a sail,
Take a glider, go by rail.

Take a wheelchair, take a cart,
Take a butt-fired super fart,
Take a hanglide from aloft,
Take sedan chairs, take a trot.
Take a sleep walk, take a prom,
Take a rickshaw from Hong Kong,
Take a snowboard, take a trek,
Take some stilts, what the heck.
Take a pumpkin coach with fairies,
Take a milkfloat from the dairy,
Take a pair of rollerskates,
Take piggy-backs on all your mates.
Take journeys that don't use a car.
Take stock if you should go that far.
Take heed when travelling here and there.
Take choices that will save our air.

Recycle Me

Recycle me into …

A super-rubbish-hero who eats all trash in sight.

The deepest deep-sea plughole to stem the oceans' rise.

An enormous sticking plaster to heal the ozone layer.

The latest spray from all the ads to oust polluted air.

A deluge-drinking monster that slurps up floods at will.

Or a heavy-duty sponge to soak up tanker spills.

Some cool device to average out the climate's sweats and shivers.

A massive ten-headed toilet brush to scrub out streams and rivers.

The world's first lap-top time machine to recycle all my hours.

An eight-sailed wind-powered turbine for all my daily power.

A giant sucking Hoover to vacuum up the gunk.

A spread-on vanishing magic gel that clears away the junk.

The greatest wildlife telly host who presents the planet's plight.

Someone who can save the world before my tea tonight.

Poo Power

In England's green and pleasant land,
Find a field that's close at hand.
Choose a cud-chewing herd of cows,
That has no toilet training vows.
Wait until they've finished tea,
Collect their dung and all their pee.
Stick the cowpats in a tank,
Hold your breath 'cause it smells mank.
Put a lid on firm and tight,
Stir the slurry every night.
Heat it to ninety-five degrees,
Until well curdled and sludgy.
Whistle a time-passing sweet refrain,
As bacterial bugs create methane.
Which, as you know, is biogas
Your cows have made from eating grass.
So now you've solved the 'moo-ted' question
Of anaerobic tank digestion –
A fancy term for making fuel
Not from crude oil but from a stool!
So entertain your friends for hours,
Turning poo into power.

"You might want to give that a few minutes."

Green Queen

When the green queen's court processes through the city,
There'll be no gold, no jewelled robes, nothing that is pretty.

The queen and all her entourage will ride on ten green mares.
Her solar-powered coach will glide alongside four green hares.

The crown she'll wear is fashioned from recycled cans of cola.
And when she smiles, you will see that ring-pulls fill her molars.

Her cloak will be a hand-me-down of purest rag and tat,
With collars made of fur-shed hairs lost by her ginger cat.

The sceptre that she proudly holds was once a fishing rod.
A buckled brooch upon her breast – the prince's dead i-Pod.

The necklace slung around her neck is made of orange pips.
Her perfume wafting through the crowds – the scent of refuse tips.

Her wind-powered wave of hand and arm is fuelled by royal whim.
The throng throw forth organic beans and sing the national hymn:

All hail the queen, the queen of green
The greenest of the green.
All hail the queen of all that's green
All hail the greenest queen!

My Natural History

I took the path by the factory
Flanked by industrial towers.
I saw no cloud, no tree, no beast,
No fish, no bird, no flower.

I took the path through the smoke stacks,
Hazy with vapour and smog.
I saw no bee, no butterfly,
No squirrel on a log.

I took the path to the city streets,
I saw no smiling face,
No playful run or leap or hop,
No playground game or race.

I took the path by the highway
Where my heartbeat could not be heard.
The bustle of life was full volume,
Overpowering whisper or word.

I took the path where the wild things are,
I laughed with the crow and the frog.
I danced in a glade of bluebells
With the dandelion and dock.

I took the path to deep woodland,
Through mazes of bramble and weed.
I wandered a track that ended
At a jungle of bracken and reed.

And there at the heart of wilderness,
Like a lost or hidden child,
Were the roots of my natural history:
What it was like to be wild.

Famous and Infamous Footprints

First creature that crept to land from the brine.

Dinosaur ones in the fossils of time.

First baby kick on the wall of the womb.

First human stride in lava or stone.

The claim of new land by an intrepid sole.

The snowshoe track that reached the Pole.

Hillary's heel on Everest's peak.

Hollywood stars foot-printing concrete.

First foot to float in the frontier of space.

The gold-medal-toe in a world record race.

The diver who first walked the bed of an ocean.

Neil Armstrong's boot setting moon dust in motion.

If Adam walked Eden, his foot in the garden.

Humankind's clodhopping footprint of carbon.

Overgreen

When waking in the dead of night,
I tell the stars,
'Switch off the lights.'

From the window on my landing,
I tell all space,
'Stop expanding.'

As I long for sleep divine,
I tell the moon,
'Dim your shine.'

And if I had a solar meeting,
I'd tell the sun,
'Turn down the heating.'

Furthermore I'd urge my daughter,
Remind the oceans,
'Don't waste water.'

But when I rest again in bed
With green thoughts racing through my head,
I dream and scheme from A to Z,
And think of all I've done and said.

It seems that I must tell the Earth
That worst of all I may have been,
Perhaps a little *overgreen.*

Street Names

The Ash Grove – now a new-build private hospital.

Bay Willow Drive – modern apartment blocks with studio rooms.

Beech Tree Avenue – detached homes with swimming pools.

The Poplars – a mansion built by celebrities.

Birch Tree Close – fine brick semis with brown-blocked drives.

Hawthorn Way – construction site for a carpet store.

The Pines – a shopping mall with a multi-storey.

Oak Tree View – the only view a factory.

Holly Bush Lane – the entrance to a retail site.

Cherry Tree Hill – anything but a cherry on the top.

What's in a name?

Street names: places named after the trees that once lived there.

On my Bike

On my bike at the traffic lights
I'm side by side with a four by four.
The driver looks at my rickety wheels,
Hasn't he seen a bike before?

Probably once he had a trike,
With stabilisers when he was five!
But now, in dull commuter land,
His life is fuelled on drive drive drive.

Then I think…
Could it be that him in there
Somehow thinks he's got the share
Of carbon grot that would be spare
From any car I might have owned?

His grand solution:
Use someone else's unused pollution.

Whose Place is it Anyway?

The golden mole is threatened by the workings of a mine.
The pine marten and polecat live on borrowed time.
Hippos cannot hide from illegal poachers' guns.
Do the cheetahs of Botswana watch their last setting suns?

As Arctic ice dissolves and polar bears decline,
Can the wolves of Ethiopia trust humankind?
Will the whitetip shark and angel shark avoid the fishing trawl?
How soon until the Mpingo tree takes its final fall?

The manta ray is troubled by pollution of the waters,
While cats of the Andes scarper from a slaughter.
Will the jaguar outrun the hunter's cold pursuit?
Can we save our ponds for the great crested newt?

Will snakes find their lairs as habitat turns to road?
Does a parking lot come first or the Puerto Rican toad?
Will koalas in their hollows survive the ruthless logging?
Shall we bother to find out or is that just too much slogging?

Why don't we remember those with whom we share the Earth?
And why won't we honour and value their true worth?
We can't let our best friends simply vanish without trace,
So let's work together and restore their rightful place.

Blue Planet's Blue

Boo hoo hoo hoo,
Blue planet's blue.

Buckets of tears,
Tsunami is here.

Weep rant and wail,
Rhinos for sale.

Cry baby cry,
Forests will die.

Howl, yelp and screech,
Oil on the beach.

Watery eyes,
Sea levels rise.

Sob, sigh and whine,
Wildlife on the line.

Sighs and lamenting,
Climate is changing.

Sing a blue song,
Habitats gone.

Boo hoo hoo hoo,
Blue planet's real blue.

Hullabaloo,
It's all up to you!

Conversation Scraps

Lolly wrapper: Hey. How'd you get here?

Cardboard tube: Came in a wheelie.

Lolly wrapper: Black one?

Cardboard tube: Yes. And you?

Lolly wrapper: Wouldn't be seen in nothing less than a green bin.

Cardboard tube: So what're you going to be recycled into?

Lolly wrapper: I want to come back as one of those posh
wedding invitation cards. With the gold all around the edges.

Cardboard tube: You've got ideas beyond your stationery.

Lolly wrapper: What about you?

Cardboard tube: I'd come back as one of those flimsy wavy sheets you get in
boxes of chocolates. All brown and shiny.

Lolly wrapper: Wouldn't want to be shut up in a box all day. Bad enough being in a bin.

Cardboard tube: Hey here we go. They're going to tip us into that pile of...

Lolly wrapper: No. Not scrap paper.

Cardboard tube: Looks like you'll come back as one of those green recycled notebooks that
kids' parents think it's cool to buy them in science museums.

Lolly wrapper: Could be worse.

Cardboard tube: How?

Lolly wrapper: Looks like you're heading to the tub for recycled loo paper.

Cardboard tube: Yuk.

Reading Matter

Icebergs: a continent's exiles,
Drifting paragraphs and sentences,
Water-bound subplots,
Lost pages of fiction floating beneath
Glaciers: frozen dialogues promising action.
Blank interleaving snowscapes,
Icy interruptions between

The metre of mountains:
Peak cloud peak cloud peak cloud,
Prefaced by sea and snowfields – long rambling chapters of punctuation:
The seal comma;
The skua's flight – a bold underline;
The breaching hump-back – arched as a question;
The calvings of ice –
Exclamations as we page-turn Antarctica.

We browse and inhale
The odour of blank sheets of snowscapes
Rule-lined by penguins.
Now tourist and trekker will footprint
Each day-breaking landscape.
Finger on shutter, they'll thumbprint each page
By marking the spot
With a digital print.

Skimming,
Scanning,
Speed reading and skipping to Antarctica's closing chapter.
The narrative is somehow
Tailed with a twist.
Or have we twisted the tale,
Creased the last page,
And cornered the cover of wilderness?

The Board of Butterflies at the Annual Moth Meeting

The High Brown Fritillary announced to the meeting,
'There are none of us left – we took a real beating.
The heathlands and wetlands are being reclaimed,
We're now reduced to only our name.'

'Pesticides, chemicals – what shall we do?'
Was the dire agenda of the Large Blue.
'Where will we breed? Please tell me and how?
Our flower-rich pastures are under the plough.'

The Marsh Mallow Moth was next to complain,
'The hedgerows are going on many a lane.'
'And what shall I do?' cried the old Brown Hairstreak,
'My home was torn down – I barely can speak.'

The Dark Bordered Beauty shed a few tears,
'New housing and industry is what we fear.'
The Barberry Carpet was also bereft,
'We have only nine breeding sites left.'

The Large Tortoiseshell said, 'It's a disgrace.
Time was I was seen in many a place.'
'Me too,' said the Straw Belle, the rare grassland moth,
'We fell to the farmer – his blade and his wrath.'

The Large Copper spoke of the bad schemes of men,
And the Black-veined Moth of the drainage of fens.
The Dark Crimson Underwing wondered who might
Take on the moths' and the butterflies' plight.

Screwed Up

I'm a screwed up piece of litter
Looking for a mate,
And any kind of homely bin
Where we can propagate.

That's a reasonable ambition
For a piece of paper scrap,
Until you find the human race
Is standing in your path.

I'm tossed from drain to pavement
And places in between,
Sometimes I'm blown about so much
I end up where I've been.

No one seems to bother,
No one seems to care,
Who could I complain to
As they kick me in the air?

People walk straight past me,
They never take a look,
Even those who tread on me
Won't pick me up.

Perhaps I'll never make it
To that papier-mâché home,
And like my mate the cardboard box
I'll roam the streets alone.

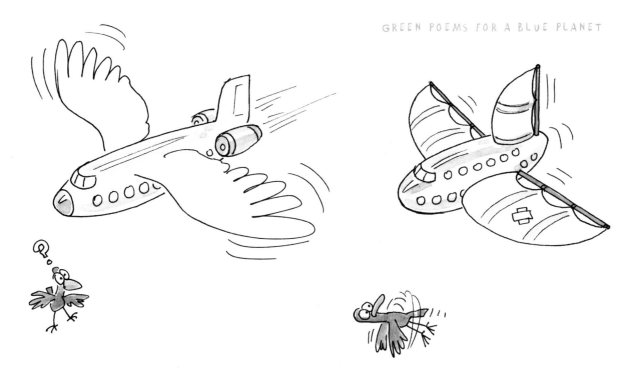

How to Make Aeroplanes Green

Paint them green with the slogan 'Hmmm. Makes you think doesn't it?'

Pilots to toss a coin. Heads we take off – tails, stay at home.

All endangered species to fly first-class back to their original habitat.

Stewards must generate wind power when giving safety demonstrations.

In-flight shops to sell organic cream teas. No watches. No bling.

First and business class to be made into allotments. No sleeping, only digging.

In-flight movies on composting.

Pick your own strawberries and raspberries on all long-haul flights.

Recycle all in-flight mags into sun hats when landing in tropical climes.

Store nothing in the overhead compartments.

Lose weight before you travel.

Order the vegetarian meal.

Remove wings and add sails. Find port to start voyage.

Get your local volcano to create an ash cloud.

Fly less.

Green Star Sheriff

He's a greenstar sheriff from the wild Wild West,
His shirt is made of cotton and he doesn't wear a vest.
His shooter, spurs, and rifle were recycled long ago.
His Stetson's in the charity shop – donated don't you know.
The sheriff loves his refried beans piled high upon a plate,
Until his chaps and waistcoat slowly self-inflate.
His horse is in a respite ranch and eats all things organic,
Equestrian yoga every day prevents all stress and panic.
His horsey liberation group has banned the rodeo,
And he'll speedcam every stagecoach that ignores his new 'go slow'.
In the saloon he fans the air with cards from games of poker –
His word is law on clean air zones; he kicks out all the smokers.
His slogan 'green not gunfights' is the sermon that he preaches,
And 'cactus solidarity' – the politics he teaches.
He's a greenstar sheriff from the wild Wild West,
With a golden piece of starfruit pinned to his chest.

Diary of a Cod

Sunday: Swam around. Called in on Jo and her five million roe. Five million kids to bring up and keep track of. No doubt most of them won't make it. Cod sob story. Swam around some more.

Monday: Swam around. Read article about the increase in world population. And the demand for me – how those protein junkies up there need more of us. Got pretty depressed about that so swam some more.

Tuesday: Got up. Had breakfast. Swam around. Found a shipwreck. Would be nice to see more of that lot down here.

Wednesday: Swam around. Got lost. Big net came down. Tried to escape. Before I knew it, I was losing speed. In seconds I was in the net and on my way up to the boat above. Some big guys in blinding yellow suits threw me about as if I was some kind of limp squid. Not even the great Cod could help me now. And even if there is a great Cod, I thought, he or she is probably fish fingers by now.

Thursday: Couldn't swim around. Was laid flat out. Freezing cold – every fin paralysed. Stuck in a box of ice alongside loads of my dead mates. Apart from being freaky it was boring. Couldn't even see out of the window of the van we were in. Couldn't see anyway because I was dead. But was having an 'out of cod' experience so I could write this.

Friday: Ouch. Got my head chopped off. And my tail. Some ripper with a knife sliced my belly. Humans shouldn't get away with that. Where are the police these days? Ended up shacked up with a pile of dead potatoes. All chopped up they were. Then, if ever a fish could drown, I was covered in ketchup, vinegar and curry sauce. Then it went dark. Someone wrapped me up. I guessed this was the end. But no. There was worse to come. I got eaten.

Saturday: Don't swim or exist. I guess you could say that doesn't matter. Plenty more fish in the sea?

Green Bedtime

Get into organic cotton jim-jams.
Enter cosily insulated bathroom,
Switch on energy-saving light bulb.
Open bar of natural soap with biodegradable wrapper,
Plug sink, half fill, wash face.

Grab toothbrush made from recycled computers.
Add one hundred percent natural minty toothpaste.
Brush and rinse with filtered water
From seventy per cent recycled glass.

Walk to bedroom in slippers with soles of old tyres.
Switch on air purifier.
Sit at desk and draw with retractable pen made from sustainable wood.
Lie down in warm bed sheets made by non-exploited workers in a foreign land.
Crank up my wind-up radio,
Or listen to a track on solar-powered mp3 player.

Hang on…
There's just one green thing I forgot to do…
Sit on my waterless composting toilet.

Mountain

I climbed past the ones from the best fashion shops,
That used to be home to trousers and tops.
I climbed through the ones that once carried shoes,
And those that had travelled a million queues.

I climbed past the white ones all flimsy and ripped,
That used to wrap takeaways, pizzas and chips.
I climbed over those that protected new books,
And those that designers had given good looks.

I arrived at the summit and stood on the top.
I erected my flag at exactly that spot.
Yet how pointless to think that I'd reached the peak,
This plastic bag mountain would be higher next week.

Greensleeves

Sing to the original tune of the traditional 'Greensleeves'

Alas, my love I'm so cheesed off,
You've dumped me for a greener guy.
And only for the reason that
His solar panels will warm you.

Chorus:

Greensleeves was all my joy,
Greensleeves was my delight.
I really organically fancy you,
Recycle your love for me Greensleeves.

I failed to make you a compost heap.
I caused the leak in your water butts.
What's worse is I couldn't stop eating meat,
And I drove to work last Tuesday.

I could not give you a wind turbine
Nor harness the power of waves for you.
The eggs I gave you were not free range
And I never put veg in the right bin.

I would give you a ring of twigs,
A dress of sunbeams, a veil of rain.
With an energy-efficient honeymoon
We'd stay in bed for a fortnight.

Greensleeves, farewell, adieu,
For I am still your lover true.
I know you would wed the environment
But maybe our love is renewable?

Global Warning Morning

It was one of those days.
Started off as normal.

But going downstairs,
The stair carpet was soggy,
Squishing and squelching.

I opened the kitchen door…

The central heating was on full.
So baking hot – tropical it was.
And, in the microclimate of the kitchen,
Those greenhouse gases had trapped the
sun's energy –
Water vapour and carbon dioxide everywhere.
Talk about a hot-spot!
Mum was in her bikini,
Dad was in his trunks,
The cat was heat-stroked.

To make matters worse,
The freezer thawed.
There was water everywhere.
Dave the hamster didn't make it –
No matter how hard he pedalled his wheel –
His cage submerged.
And, like the *Titanic*,
Was doomed to a watery grave.
Poor Dave.

Disaster!
The milk had risen to the edge of my cereal bowl.
Then it leapt and swept up every knife,
Fork and spoon off the table.
No amount of dishcloths, tea towels,
Mops or buckets would stem the flow
Of waves from this cereal tsunami.
One big flood.
I could see that soon
The kitchen would no longer exist,
Or the house,
Or the street.

Yet outside…
All the neighbours were still trying to rev their cars
Out of the deluge –
To get to work, to school, to the shops.
No one took any notice.
It was just another of those
Global warning mornings.

When Earth is Full

When Earth is full of all my trash
Where else can it go?
Blast it off to space or Mars,
Who will ever know?

Drop it in a black hole,
No one will know it's there.
Or on a passing comet,
Who would give a care?

Send it off to Dr. Who,
I'll give him my solution.
Take it to some alien world
That won't mind our pollution.

Journey to another age,
Travel back in time,
Dump it with the dinosaurs,
They won't know it's mine.

Orbit it around the Earth,
For a thousand years or more,
Until it all comes crashing down,
At someone else's door.

What about the universe?
There's lots of room out there.
It can't all really stay down here,
That just isn't fair.

And what about the Big Bang?
The very start of time.
That would take a bin or two,
Or maybe eighty-nine.

But here's the thought I'm thinking,
Which could be quite a blow.
When the universe is full of trash,
Where *else* can it go?

Signed Sealed and Delivered

To whom it may concern,

Was minding my own business when a five hundred billion-ton ice shelf fell on my head.

What are you going to do about it?

Leo. P. Ardseal

Greenophobia

The fear I'll travel less.
The fear of sorting all my waste.
The fear of paying for my carbon mess.
The fear of sitting in a smaller car.
The fear that by getting involved things might change.
The fear of turning green.

Torboy's Boot

I am driving. Dartmoor bound.
Storm clouds ahead – black and solid as iron.
Wipers are welcome beats:
Rhythm in this mass of Jaguar and Audi spray.
Miles beyond…the hope of stars and sleep.

Daybreak dares to break my slumber.
Dressed and bundled, packed and braced, I bear my son.
Torwards we trek – outstaring bulls and striding streams.
I call him Torboy:
The weather-beaten centre stone of parenthood.

When the journey tor and back is done,
My bootless babe dismounts.
Sock-sodden, frozen-footed on the left,
He lolls and limps along;
His right is snow-capped Wellington.

I must go back.
This time no challenge or the winter view.
It's for the boot somewhere plastic-poised on ancient soil.
Again the sleet and streams for father's feet.
Past the bull, the tumbled tree,
The icy dung, the silent spruce.

Where is that piece of twenty-first century blue?
Non-bio footprint of the New Year's hike –
The colour of the Torboy's wind-chapped hue.
Ponies – the markers for my tracks have moved.
And on descent – a reverie – which will outlast?
Tor or boot?

Environmentally Friendly Skipping Rhyme

Give me one give me two,
Save an otter in Peru.
Give me two give me three,
For a monkey puzzle tree.
Give me three give me four,
Stop an iceberg from a thaw.
Give me four give me five,
Keep an elephant alive.
Give me five give me six,
Protect an eagle and its chick.
Give me six give me seven,
For endangered Woma pythons.
Give me seven give me eight,
Help a rhino find a mate.
Give me eight give me nine,
Giant pandas on the line.
Give me nine give me ten,
Saving my environment.

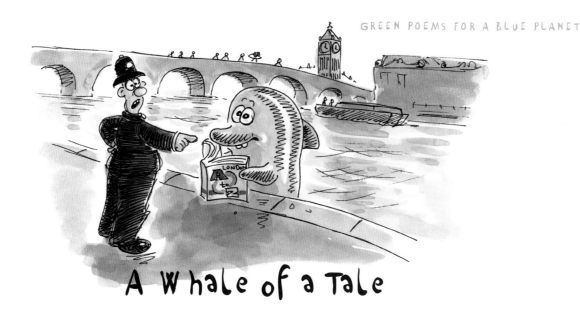

A Whale of a Tale

Once upon a time a Bottlenose Whale,
(Searching for squid in the deep North Sea),
Distracted by rig noise, explosions, or sonar,
Was sent off course – and this is her tale.

Like a fairytale child alone in the woods,
The eleven-year-old lost her way.
Forty miles up the Thames to the shallows
she wandered –
And floundered on Battersea's riverbank mud.

A man on a train double-took twice;
That's four times he peered at the murky green waters.
Once more at the fin, then three taps on his mobile –
A whale of a tale to tell the police?

The whale swam upstream and swish-slapped her tail
As her bulk passed the Houses of Parliament.
Was the blow from her spout for the onlookers there
A solo petition for the plight of the whale?

In minutes the water turned brown with blood
As the rocks of the river pierced the whale's skin.
Then numerous vets, medics and divers,
Waded towards her and did all they could.

If only the song of the whale could be played
From the mouth of the river to call her back home.
But such notions were futile since boats on the Thames
Drowned any music the scientists made.

Now the river was low for a mammal so large,
So rescuers attached her to floating pontoons.
Until, like a baby in blanket and harness,
She was hoisted by crane onto a barge.

The team feared the worst: she was in much pain;
Too heavy when out of her watery home.
And stressed by the mayhem and clamour of London,
She died amidst sounds of sirens and planes.

So remember *Hyperoodon ampullatus*
Also known as the Bottlenose Whale.
She hadn't intended to visit London,
But visit she did, and that was her tale.

*On Saturday January 21st 2006, after veering off course
and ending up in the Thames, the whale is reported
to have died at about 7pm despite all attempts to
save her. Her remains are now in the Natural History
Museum Scientific Research Collection, England.*

Energy Laugh

What energy is musical?
So *La* Energy.

What energy is rude?
Wind.

What energy is friendly?
Wave energy.

Which energy is wave energy's friend?
Hi! dropower.

Which energy can be grown?
A power plant.

What is green, has petals, two wheels, handlebars, and goes round and round?
A recycling plant.

Why did the chicken stop in the road?
She ran out of henergy!

What did the green TV say to the non-green TV?
Don't just standby and do nothing.

How many environmentalists does it take to change an energy-saving light bulb?
None. They're saving their energy.

Damn!

Rivers:
The Earth's lifelines –
Dammed or poisoned with waste –
Agricultural, industrial.

The Jordan: Israel's holy river,
Once deep and wide,
Was the place where babies bathed –
Where Jesus was baptised.
Now no more than a sewage pool
Below the Sea of Galilee.

Rivers:
Blocked by dams.
These feats of engineering prowess
Change the way our rivers shape the planet,
Disorient migrating creatures, displace our
                                      population,
Split our eco-systems, curtail the salmon run.

Take the mighty Colorado:
Great red river that forgot how it once flowed
As smooth as blood through the Grand Canyon.
Now not a drop reaches the delta.
Las Vegas and Tucson drain it dry
For the Strip's fountains and swimming pools.

Or take the Rio Grande – or rather don't.
For it, the sea is but a distant memory.
Like a thirsty child,
Parched El Paso gulps its waters,
And leaves dribbles in its riverbed.

Rivers:
Crystal-moving molecules that,
Once upon a time,
Freely flowed from source to sea.
Unimpeded, they began their journeys high –
From a mountain source.
Then other friendly waters joined them –
Streams and springs, cascades and falls –
Like children wild at play –
They ran a natural course, not one of obstacles.

Rivers:
Dammed, drained, polluted, re-routed.
Damn!

Upwardly Mobile?

Time to upgrade my mobi again
To …
Tri-bands and quad–bands,
Downloads of boybands,
SIM cards stuffed with my ten thousand mates,
Video calling, voice mail and e-mail,
Predictive texts about all of my dates.

The next one must have
Enhanced user interface,
Wi-fi and Bluetooth,
New USBs,
Connectivity heaven
To transfer files quickly,
From boyfriend to girlfriend,
From business to home.

Increased functionality
Has to be cool,
'cause my mates have got speakerphones, ringtones and games.
I need to have millions and trillions of pixels,
Video capture and digital zoom.

Or what about a Blackberry –
Sounds so friendly doesn't it?
'Ah … Blackberry.'
Perhaps we'll bake a pie for two?
'Try my Blackberry and Apple pie.'
We can eat it and e-mail and surf as we chew.

Next year half the world
Will carry a mobile.
And for those who discard and upgrade – a thought:
Most phones will work for a few years.
Is it really time to upgrade my mobi?

It's a Scream being Green

It's a scream being green,
All covered in puke,
Dribbling with snot,
And bits of lime slime,
Dripping with horrible,
Swampy wet weed,
Stringy and wrapping
A heart full of moss,
Pumping a dark olive goo
Thick as glue,
Under a slithery gunge-grassy skin
Peeling with patches of mouldy old scabs.

So apart from the ugly hue of my bulk,
It's a scream being green
For a monstrous hulk.

Fruit Miles

Boxes, bags, packs and bunches,
Piles and piles of long-hauled fruit –
Flown en masse from other countries –
Stacked on supermarket shelves.

Medjool dates grown on the West Bank
Chilean cherries, Brazilian limes,
Californian pistachios, pomegranates, grapefruits,
Spanish sun-soaked clementines.

Columbian physalis, Italian kiwis,
Fresh strawberries from the land of the Nile,
New Zealand apricots, South American melons,
Jet-lagged bananas of the Windward Isles.

South African lychees, passion fruit, peaches,
Costa Rican pineapple, Portugese pears.
Israeli Sharon fruit, oranges, lemons,
Red grapes, green grapes, golden plums.

The fruit is green but not its journey –
Miles and miles across the globe.
Only a pile of Cox's apples
Came from an orchard down the road.

*On checking the boxes of fruit in a supermarket,
I discovered that all the fruit except for English
Cox's apples had travelled miles across the world
to reach the shelves.*

Bioverse

I'm a bioverse poet with biodiverse verse.
What could be better? What could be worse?
If I wrote you a poem and took out some words –
Would it work? Would it scan? Could you read it aloud?
How would you know what it's really about?
An example: a line with a few words amiss –
The set the of sea.
The set the of sea?
Is nonsense to me.

A much better line is, I'm sure you'll agree,
'Pink sunlight set over blue waves of the sea.'
Every word has its partner, the vowel length sublime,
The line doesn't waver in metre or time.
Each verb has an adverb, each noun has its place,
They make up the whole, like the parts of a face.

But the reason I'm working on being so witty,
Is to compare what I write here to biodiversity.
Imagine it as evolution's rhyme –
The variety of life – tales told over time
Of rivers, forests, grasslands and seas,
Deserts and prairies, coral reefs,
Animals, plants, fungi and genes,
Microbes to whales and all in between.
The millions of species each other sustain,
Quite a tall order for mankind to attain.

So take note of my stanzas of bioverse verse,
If I take out a bit –
It simply gets worse.
The poem will not function when read or recited,
Nor will the Earth if its systems are blighted.
If one thing's removed through destruction or greed,
Biodiversity's ode is not such a good read.

Ballad of the Green Patient

Why am I in a hospital bed?

You were found unconscious in a compost heap.

Why have I got a broken leg?

You slipped on rechargeable batteries.

Why have I got a broken arm?

You were entwined and trapped in a 'bag for life'.

Why have I got four cracked ribs?

A big green wheelie hit you hard.

Why am I wheezing and gasping for breath?

You almost drowned in a water butt.

Why have I got a fractured skull?

A solar panel crashed down on your head.

Why is my skin cut and bruised?

You fell into a bottle bank.

Will I ever get out of here?

Yes, when the bin truck comes on Wednesday.

Can Opener

A Connecticut cannery of cantankerous canners –
Canoodling can merchants and canny can-mongerers –
Can cans for delivery to all Canucopia.
Can you believe it – canillions of cans all over the world?
From Canada's can stores to Cancun's cantinas,
Can-opened cans of canned cannelloni,
Sweet cob-stripped corn and Cantonese rice,
Are cooked by a cordon-bleu chef
Into this meal and that one and cancan-shaped canapés.
Cantonese-corn-cannelloni grilled canapés?
Can't imagine the taste or the texture, can you?
But cans of a candied canteloup fizz,
Alongside the food,
Are not only consumed at candlelit dinners
Or in dreary canteens of canal-side cafés;
But by campers at fires and walkers at picnics
And those in the wilds with their rafts and canoes.
And even by cantering tourists from Cannes,
Canterbury, Canberra, or the Canaries
Who open their cans beneath canted canvasses
Out in the canyons where cans can't be canned.
Let's hope that these can-possessed gobblers and drinkers
Don't empty their minds as they empty their cans,
For the cans that they've opened and can't then dispose of –
Can often be dumped in the bush, woods or beaches.
Much better is filling a 'backpack-come-trashcan'
To take home for crushing, collecting, compacting,
Candescent melting to chill back to can.

When I walk in the wilds
I often take note that
Some can't be bothered.
Some bothered, can.

Spikes

Three rusty spikes –
Relics of a war or fishing craft –
Lay buried in the crests of Welsh green waves.

Low tide.
Emerged erect.
Each prong of Neptune's fork a throw apart.
This sea-stained metal has a starfish hue and driftwood brown which,
Against the failing light and shifting sands, isn't found.

I saw a breeze-bent body boarder stroke across these needle points.
'Hey you out there!' I cried, 'that's where the danger lies.'
The boy swam on.
My words were lost in wind and water, break and gull.

Wetsuit zipped, I raced towards the flow which swept the boy towards the spikes.
Too late to turn, he flailed his arms as iron struck his flimsy form.
He couldn't make the turn – a rusty shard had gashed his leg.

Each swoosh I dived and grabbed the boy.
We sailed to shore as safe as surf.
Yet not in fathoms, but an inch deep in the sand, were spikes in miniature:
Shore-line spines of weever fish.
As sharp as razor-light, they pierced my foot.

Impaled, I felt the toxic pin-pricked pain,
As boy and man were carried up the coastal path –
The boy for soothing balm, the man for hotel bath,
Where scalding water bathed my toe
And poison from my seaborne foe dispersed.

Later we drank tea with buttered scones,
While breaking news of shipwrecks on the coast of Wales
Changed the complexion of our ills.
Attacks from iron scrap or fin-fired bayonets are better still than tanker spills.

Who's Holding the Ball?

The pitch was once green, pristine and green.
Until …
To the roar of the crowd, from out of the tunnel,
Came humankind's team –
A frightening formation of billions of players
With one aim in mind: to control the ball.

The whistle was blown.
The boots hit the ball,
Kicked it around, rolled it in dirt, ripped up the turf.
The team tackled hard one on another –
Possession their tactic –
Keeping the ball firm at their feet,
Where they felt it belonged.

Now imagine the world as a football in play –
With the studprints of commerce, consumption, pollution,
Exploitation and greed stamped on the ball.
Visible logos of overlooked fouls.

When the whistle is blown for the end of the match –
There are no extra minutes for injury time.
The ball is deflated –
Punctured below in Antarctica's air,
And further atop at the North Pole.

What shall we do then?
Wait for a ref to penalty shoot it out into space?
It might even land on a planetary world
Where an alien race will pick up the ball
For their football museum's soccer exhibit.

And maybe they'll label it 'This was once Earth.'
In a match score that ended
Humanity Ununited 1 Earth 0.

I'm Dreaming of a Green Christmas

I'm dreaming of a green Christmas,
With each recycled card I write.
No wrapping paper,
Or cardboard boxes,
I'll even cut down on the lights.

I'm dreaming of a green Christmas,
My presents will be second-hand.
I'll make toilet tube crackers,
Cook gingerbread fairies,
And let all turkeys roam the land.

I'm dreaming of a green Santa,
Whose reindeer don't poo in the sky.
He'll present all houses,
With solar panels –
And only eat low-fat mince pies.

I'm dreaming of a green Christmas,
I'll buy a tree to plant outside.
Pine cones and berries
For decorations,
I'll feel so self-satisfied.

I'm dreaming of a green Christmas,
I'll ride by sledge and not by car.
I'll sing green-themed carols,
And why watch telly?
When I can watch the Christmas stars.

The Last E-Mail on Earth

Date: Friday (sometime in the future)

This e-mail has been returned. Recipients not found.

To: contact@isthereactuallyanyonestilloutthere.com

Re: Biocide

Now that we have irreversibly destroyed the planet through the destruction of Earth's life systems and the processes on which all life depends…

Any ideas?

Yours,

Humankind

Given no-one is here to respond to this e-mail. Updating your anti-virus settings.

Bean Beaten

Thirteen barrels of Benzene,
Spewing over polythene.
Fourteen million magazines,
Piled on top of old latrines.
Fifteen thousand smashed machines,
Under sixteen mezzanines.
Seventeen hundred submarines,
Dumped with eighteen limousines.
Nineteen thousand and two tureens,
Bouncing on trashed trampolines.
A further thousand junked widescreens,
Squashing umpteen tambourines.
The total waste of nothing green,
Flattening fields of soya beans.

Ode to Broccoli

Hey bro, you're the cute dude I love –
Broccoli: cabbage plant of old,
Your flower heads, your leaves, your stalks,
Stemmed fleshy branches, green and wild
Are greater than Manhattan's sights.
The London Eye should be replaced
With broccoli for all to ride.

And though you are Italian
Da Vinci never painted you –
And worse he never knew the truth –
The Mona Lisa only smiles
Because she ate you with a round
Or two or three of runner beans.

Every band should make a download:
'Broc me baby, you heart broccer'–
Songs about the late white sprouting,
Early purple or green comet.
Varieties to top the charts.

You should be honoured as Doc. Broc
For services to medicine.
Your anti-viral properties
And disease-busting chemicals
Are hailed by vegetarians
Who, across the known green universe,
With every cabbage, kale and brussel sprout,
Calabrese and cauliflower –
Recite this ode:

Listen to my flow.
Listen to my flow.
Give me five, give me five.
Give me five florets bro.

Venice Graffiti

It wasn't like this last time.
Now the bridges and the walls,
Calle, campo, canal and church,
The concertina shutters of the shops,
Have spray can fresco-texts as random as a swirling cappuccino froth
Or flights of pigeon flocks.

Rivalling the Guggenheim and Biennale's abstract art,
The park's 'treeffitied' barks are tattooed with
Signatures – as neat as vaporetti trails;
Underlines – black streaks like fleeting gondolas;
Exclamation marks – as bold as St. Mark's campanile;
Anything the tree may have to say has gone –
Ranted, raved and shouted down
With the angst of aerosol.

At Vivaldi's Ospedale,
Echoes of *Four Seasons* –
Spring green, summer gold, autumn brown and winter white,
As mad as music manuscript,
Colour splash the walls with scribed and scribbled politics.
Yet when this city in another time
Is seabed bound by Neptune's watery noose,
It may be found by voyagers: a future Marco Polo or a Cabot
Diving deep through wave-erased Tintorettos and Bellinis –
To stones with painted tales as vibrant as the toppings on a pizza crust:
'Carlo loves Emanuela';
'Americans – leave Iraq';
'Government lies – conspiracy'.

Graffiti –
So fitting that the word is Italian.

Italy has a major graffiti problem – with many of the walls of its streets, canals and churches now covered in spray-can rants.

Post-Nuke Blues

Well I woke up this morning, I was feeling like a dog.
Yeah I woke up this morning, I was feeling like a dog.
Don't wanna go outside into that ash and choking smog.

I've got the post-nuke blues,
Apathy shuffle in my shoes.
I got the post-nuke blues,
Apathy shuffle in my shoes
I thought I'd saved the world, but man I never knew.

Raised my head up from my pillow, strangest sight I ever saw.
Raised my head up from my pillow, strangest sight I ever saw.
A nuclear reactor's core blasted through my bedroom door.

Gonna take a shower, gonna get myself real clean.
Gonna take a real hot shower, get myself all squeaky clean.
Gonna scrub off that pollution that makes my pores so black and mean.

I stared into the mirror, I was looking pretty weird.
Stared into that mirror, I was looking pretty weird.
I thought I looked a bit absurd with my radioactive beard.

I looked out of my window, there was nothing I could see.
Looked right out of that window, there was nothing I could see.
No person, bus, no cat, no car, no house, no plant or tree.

Gonna play my mean piano and write me a new verse.
Gonna play that mean piano and write me a new verse.
Well I wished I'd written greens not blues – I might have saved the Earth.

Tree Library

A million books.
A trillion pages.
Once a wood, a forest, trees.
Until those towering friendly giants
Sacrificed their bodies.
As if some lumberjack librarian called in
These gentle edifices as overdue.

Now we write life narratives on their flesh.
Perhaps a fiction or a pithy poem.
We never waited by the tree –
Alive and vital –
To hear what story it might tell
When its wind-splayed branches reached down to us –
As if a grandfather
Who would tell a tale.

Song Sung Round

Chicks that learn their song,
Learn first in part and then the whole.
When learnt in full,
It's said they 'sing it round'.
Now they are equipped to serve their flock –
To sing their melody
In harmony with all the Earth.
What about our song?
We also learn in part,
But will we ever sing our song round?

Green Dreams

A green land:
Virid verdant fields,
Viridian grass,
Viridescent,
Vivid.

I'm running at speed.
I hear my own engine –
Beat after beat –
Repeated refrains marking the rhythms of
Light, shade, wind, rain.
I sprint through a storm –
A thunderous symphony
That rattles my bones –
Anatomy playing the music of weather.

I'm element-honed
In all shades of green –
Temporary tattoos sketched on my skin
By nature's fine hand.
I embrace sight and sound:
The honeybee's buzz;
The pattern of cattle;
The song of the thrush;
The splashing of mud;
They bond me to Earth.

Without question or warning, signal or sign,
A change of the scene –
Green turns to grey.
The fields are beneath a thick shroud of concrete.
All that was nature removed from here.
Instead, the pavements and fountains of super malls –
My worst nightmare.

How to Save Water

In a bowl
Without a hole.
In a bucket,
Don't chuck it.
With a meter
Measuring litres.
Bathe an hour?
Better shower.
Watering roses?
Not with hoses.

Pond Property

Property wanted for professional frog.

Ideally rural.

Must be in clean condition or with scope for improvement.

Exceptional jumper – could easily hop in to city centre –

May even consider a newly converted garden pond

If well proportioned and tastefully presented

Within easy reach of large kitchen/breakfast woodland area.

Private entrance and high water level (no steep sides) preferred,

Since access to land is required.

Can afford two hundred bugs a month.

Happy to share (will split rent) with mayflies, whirligig beetles, and leeches.

I should mention I'm living alone with several froglets to support –

So, close enough to amenities would be handy for takeaway insects and worms.

Property must be in the local catchment area

Of marshes, ditches, swamps, rocks and puddles.

Last pond we lived in was drained and built on –

So don't contact me if there is proximity to humans.

(Or lawnmowers. My partner met a frightful end with one).

And no noisy unfriendly neighbours: fish, birds, bats or snakes.

Don't want to croak on about it but I'm on my last legs (so to speak).

There's a big shortage of ponds out there.

No time wasters please.

Horror Movie

One foot at a time –
It crept up the staircase.
Slow as the stealth of climbing plants.

I thought I heard it.
Or did my mind play a freaky trick?
The creak or windborne gust
Might simply be a cat or dog.

But then...
Accompanied by the screeching sound of
Eeeeeeeeeeeeeeeeeek! Eerie violins.
An icy draught stole in and chilled me to the core.
My bones froze rigid,
As the weep and wail of something stirred
Outside the bedroom door.

My eyes looked down –
A camera in slow reveal –
Until they rested on the icy water
Bleeding through the threshold.

Then a mighty rip:
A special sound effect that turned my heart into a crazy drummer's beat.
Faster faster as it raised the tension...
Splinter splinter sharp sharp sharp...
Horror hacked the panels of the door.

Beaks and claws, hooves and paws came pounding through;
Perished creatures from the jungle or the forest glades –
A ghostly herd of everything once wild:
A million wilting stems of plants beheaded;
The severed limbs of fifty thousand trees;
Flocks of black-oil stricken birds.

The horror of a century's abuse had come back a'haunting.

Tiger Tiger

Tiger tiger where are you?
Lying low or lost from view?
Faint ghostly stripes flash through the night,
Black gold black gold black gold white.

Tiger tiger – once burned bright
In poems and forests of the night.
When tracks and paths felt pad of paw,
Now there's no marker of your claw.

Tiger tiger's jewelled eyes
See poachers' guns – that's no surprise.
For your fur, your bones, your skin,
Are hunted for weird medicine.

Tiger tiger torn apart,
They've taken what was once your heart.
That which made you stalk and stride
In the forests of the wild.

Tiger tiger where are you?
One of the black and golden few.
Your burning colours of the night,
Have been switched off – like a light.

Tiger tiger it's insane,
Three thousand big cats now remain.
Oh one with black and golden hue,
Where will you hide, what will you do?

Tiger tiger burning bright,
Gone from forests of the night.
Who will listen to your plight
Tiger tiger out of sight?

Bottle Billions

One plastic bottle empty in my hand,
One plastic bottle empty in my hand,
Such a bore to hold it or carry it around
Much easier to toss it or bury it underground.

Ten plastic bottles the family have drunk dry,
Ten plastic bottles the family have drunk dry,
What a drag to reuse and fill them up again,
Let's bin them and pretend we recycled all the ten.

A hundred plastic water bottles selling in a store,
A hundred plastic water bottles selling in a store,
With recycling symbols that make the buyer think,
They'll be squeaky clean and green if they buy the drink.

The truth is only a small amount gets to be recycled,
The truth is that a small percent gets to be recycled,
Why not print the cold hard figures around the bottle top?
And make us count the cost before we drink another drop.

Forty billion plastic bottles tossed into a dump,
Every year billions of bottles tossed into a dump,
To decompose the bottles could take a thousand years,
I won't be here to watch it mount so need I shed a tear?

Forty billion plastic bottles tossed into a dump,
Forty billion plastic bottles tossed into a dump,
And if forty billion bottles were all recycled… then
There'd be no more plastic tossed into the dump.

No plastic bottles tossed into a dump
No plastic bottles tossed into a dump
If they're all recycled they can be used again
To make a garden shed, a park bench, a T-shirt or a pen.

Gaia

Gaia –
What a gal!
Earth goddess,
Mother Earth of ancient myth.
Out of Chaos she appeared
Born from nothing –
As if one day she'd decided to put on a perfect dress
And venture out into the universe.
On her arm she had no need for any man.
Single-handed and strong-headed,
She reproduced and birthed the sea and sky.
So the story goes.

Another story –
Truer than that tale –
Skips thousands of years.
James Lovelock,
Scientist and lover of the Earth,
Named this planet Gaia.
In this vivacious globe-shaped figure dashing round the sun,
He saw an orb of effervescent life –
The Earth as living entity
Which, in giving life to all,
In turn was given life by her environment.
So claimed Lovelock's hypothesis.

Gaia –
Goddess Earth,
Was cherished by her learned lover.
He sang her praises and embraced her dance of life.
But sometimes lovers are not left alone.
Others, pretending that they loved her too,
Brought black bouquets of smog –
The perfumes of her errant world.
Surely she would smile to smell their scent?
Then with proud and heavy steps,
Those false lovers trod her toes –
Upsetting James' and Gaia's dance.

Envy

If the envy that I have
For that new flashy, sporty car
Zooming round a track in seconds
Could be transferred
To wishes for a greener car –
I would be green with envy!

what if?

What if the princess, turned environmental warrior, was imprisoned in an oil derrick and tortured by the heat of climate change? What if she was saved by her gallant knight in green vegetables? What if it was Sir Richard Branson on his eco-friendly transatlantic flying horse Pegavirgin? What if, armed with only a parsnip and a bunch of bananas, he had to battle the evil Lance Pollutalot from the Kingdom of Landfillonia? What if he won, rescued, and was granted the organic soap-scented hand of the princess? What if they were enthroned at the Castle de Nonemissions? What if they recycled themselves and lived happily ever after? What if they stayed up all night on endless cups of Fairtrade coffee? What if they wrote a hit song about how to change the world for the better, for the greener, for a future? What if they recorded it in a solar-powered studio and serenaded each other by the light of energy-saving light bulbs? What if Simon Cowell backed it, the whole world downloaded it, loved it, and reduced their carbon footprint? What if there were green fairytales that came true? Just what if?

Green Poem

Do it. Pick me up.
Put me down and I'm on standby.

Read me right this minute, clearly speak my text.
Do not spin my stanzas, do not tumble syllables.

Savour my organic commas, my scrumptious semi-colons,
Drink my full stops, still and fresh, from the river of a pen.

Go outside – read my words aloud.
Warm breath makes the flowers grow.

That's enough – I can go now – it doesn't worry me.
I've no need to be kept
With other books of verse:
Odes and ballads, children's rhymes, anthologies –
Left on your shelves or in libraries.

So remember…
After I'm read, I'm as good as dead.
Go on you can do it. Tear me out,
Rip me to shreds
And drop in your recycle box.

In my next life I might come back
As a Shakespeare sonnet.

IN
MEMORY
OF
GREEN
POEM
BACK AGAIN
SOON

www.martinkiszko.com
www.greenpoemsforablueplanet.com